RUBANK EDUCATIONAL LIBRARY No.

Sixteen Artistic Duets

for

Two Saxophones

by Ben Vereecken

CONTENTS

RUBANK®

HAL•LEONARD® CORPORATION

7777 W. BLUEMOUND RD. P.O. BOX 13819 MILWAUKEE, WI 53213

Twilight Shadows
WALTZ

1

Remember Me

FANTASY

S. A. D.

Thoughts at Eventide

FANTASY

S. A. D.

The Chatterers

POLKA

Trio

Two Artists
GRAND DUET DE CONCERT

Piu mosso

piu mosso e cresc.

S.A.D.

Reminiscences of Youth
ROMANCE

S.A.D.

S.A.D.

Two Butterflies

CAPRICE

S.A.D.

S.A.D.

Midgets Dance
CHARACTERISTIC

S.A.D.

S.A.D.

A Conversation

CHARACTERISTIC

The Boatmen

BARCAROLLE

S.A.D.

A Witches Frolic
CHARACTERISTIC

S.A.D.

S.A.D.

In the Days of Knights

FANTASY

Andante Cantabile

Bay of Monterey

ROMANCE

S.A.D.

S.A.D.

Memories of the Ballet

WALTZ

S. A. D.

S.A.D.

Shepherds Dance
CHARACTERISTIC

Allegro ma non troppo

S.A.D.

S.A.D.

Tenderness
DUET DE CONCERT

S.A.D.

S.A.D.